The Environment

Distinguishing Between Fact and Opinion

Curriculum Consultant: JoAnne Buggey, Ph.D.
College of Education, University of Minnesota

By William Dudley

Greenhaven Press, Inc.
P.O. Box 289009
San Diego, CA 92198-0009

Titles in the opposing viewpoints juniors series:

AIDS	The Palestinian Conflict
Alcohol	Patriotism
Animal Rights	Poverty
Death Penalty	Prisons
Drugs and Sports	Smoking
The Environment	Television
Gun Control	Toxic Wastes
The Homeless	The U.S. Constitution
Immigration	Working Mothers
Nuclear Power	Zoos

Library of Congress Cataloging-in-Publication Data

Dudley, William, 1964–
    The environment: distinguishing between fact and opinion / by
William Dudley.
       p.   cm. — (Opposing viewpoints juniors)
    Summary: Presents opposing viewpoints on four different
environmental issues.
  ISBN 0-89908-603-9
    1. Pollution—Juvenile literature. 2. Nonrenewable natural
resource—Juvenile literature. 3. Refuse and refuse disposal—
United States—Juvenile literature.   [1. Pollution.
2. Nonrenewable natural resources. 3. Natural resources. 4. Refuse
and refuse disposal.]   I. Title. II. Series.
TD176.D83   1990
363.7—dc20

90-3819
CIP
AC

Cover photo: ©1989, Martin Rogers, FPG International

CONTENTS

THE PURPOSE OF
THIS BOOK

An Introduction to
Opposing Viewpoints

When people disagree, it is hard to figure out who is right. You may decide one person is right just because the person is your friend or relative. But this is not a very good reason to agree or disagree with someone. It is better if you try to understand why these people disagree. On what main points do the two people disagree? Read or listen to each person's argument carefully. Separate the facts and opinions that each person presents. Finally, decide which argument best matches what you think. This process, examining an argument without emotion, is part of what critical thinking is all about.

This is not easy. Many things make it hard to understand and form opinions. People's values, age, and experience all influence the way they think. This is why learning to read and think critically is an invaluable skill.

Opposing Viewpoints Juniors books will help you learn and practice skills to improve your ability to read critically. By reading opposing views on an issue, you will become familiar with methods people use to attempt to convince you that their point of view is right. And you will learn to separate the authors' opinions from the facts they present.

Each Opposing Viewpoints Juniors book focuses on one critical thinking skill that will help you judge the views presented. Some of these skills are telling fact from opinion, recognizing propaganda techniques, and locating and analyzing the main idea. These skills will allow you to examine opposing viewpoints more easily. The viewpoints are placed in a running debate and are always placed with the pro view first.

What Is the Difference Between Fact and Opinion?

In this Opposing Viewpoints Juniors book you will be asked to identify and study statements of fact and statements of opinion. A fact is a statement that can be proven true. Here are some examples of factual statements: "The Statue of Liberty was dedicated in 1886 in New York," "Dinosaurs are extinct," and "George Washington was the first U.S. president." It is a fairly easy thing to prove these facts true. For instance, a historian in the year 3000 might need to prove when the Statue of Liberty was dedicated. One way she might do this is to check in the Hall of Records in New York. She would try to find a source to verify the date. Sometimes it is harder to prove facts true. And some ideas that are stated as facts may not be. In this book you will be asked to question facts presented in the viewpoints and be given some ways in which you might go about proving them.

Statements of opinion cannot be proved. An opinion is a statement that expresses how a person feels about something or what a person thinks is true. Remember the facts we mentioned? They can easily be changed into statements of opinion. For example, "Dinosaurs became extinct because a huge meteor hit the Earth," "George Washington was the best president the United States ever had," and "Rebuilding the Statue of Liberty was a waste of money," are all statements of opinion. They express what one person believes to be true. Opinions are not better than facts. They are different. Opinions are based on many things, including religious,

social, moral, and family values. Opinions can also be based on medical and scientific facts. For instance, many scientists have made intelligent guesses about other planets based on what they know is true about Earth. The only way these scientists would know their opinions were right is if they were able to visit other planets and test their guesses. Until their guesses are proved, then, they remain opinions. Some people have opinions that we do not like, or with which we disagree. That does not always make their opinions wrong—or right. There is room in our world for many different opinions.

When you read differing views on any issue, it is very important to know when people are using facts and when they are using opinions in an argument. When writers use facts, it makes their argument more believable and easier to prove. The more facts the author has, the more the reader can tell that the writer's opinion is based on something other than personal feelings.

Authors that base their arguments mostly on their own opinions, then, are impossible to prove factually true.

This does not mean that these types of argument are not as meaningful. It means that you, as the reader, must decide whether or not you agree or disagree based on personal reasons, not factual ones.

We asked two students to give their opinions on the environment issue. Examine the following viewpoints. Look for facts and opinions in their arguments.

The environment is our number one problem.

I believe that pollution is the biggest problem facing this country and the whole world. Pollution harms the air we breathe, the water we drink, and the land on which we grow our food. We have taken all of these things for granted. We have to stop abusing our planet.

The river that runs by our town used to have clean water. But then a fertilizer factory was built next to it. Now some people are afraid to swim in the river because of pollution. The factory also puts gross stuff into the air. On some days you can see a brown haze in the sky. My mother says she never saw such a thing when she was little.

More and more people move into our town every year. This is why there is so much pollution. The woods in my neighborhood used to have eagles and foxes. Now they are gone, and the woods are full of litter instead. Also, most of our forests have been chopped down to make room for new roads, shopping centers, and parking lots.

I wonder why people are doing this? I hope that people will change and work for clean air, water, and natural wilderness. I feel that by the time I am an adult, there will be nothing left.

The environment is not our number one problem.

I am getting sick and tired of people who keep complaining about the environment. They keep saying that it is the most important problem. But what about the homeless? What about drugs? What about people starving? Aren't these issues at least as important? I think so.

People complain about the factory by the river in my town. But the factory also provides good jobs. I know this because my father works there. And they are careful about keeping the environment clean. The factory managers have spent millions of dollars in equipment to make sure the river and the air stays clean. The river is still safe to swim in.

People who worry about the environment seem not to like people very much. For instance, some people in our town want to limit the number of new homes built here. That means less people can live here. Sure, this town is more populated than it used to be. But that is a good thing. What's wrong with more stores, churches, and schools? We should concentrate on making sure there are enough homes and jobs for everyone—*that* should be our number one problem.

Jim and Laura have very different opinions about the environment. Both of them use examples of fact and opinion in their arguments:

Jim:

FACTS

Some people are afraid to swim in the river.

Woods have been cut down to make new roads and shopping centers.

OPINIONS

The river is too polluted to swim in.

We take our air and water for granted.

Laura:

FACTS

The factory spends money on controlling pollution.

The town is more populated than before.

OPINIONS

The river is safe enough to swim in.

Providing jobs and homes should be a number one priority.

In this sample, both Jim and Laura give equal numbers of facts and opinions. Look at the opinions listed in this sample. Both Jim and Laura think they are right about the environment. What do you think after reading this sample? Why?

Think of two facts you know and two opinions you have about the environment.

As you continue to read through the viewpoints in this book, try keeping a tally like the one above to compare the authors' arguments.

CHAPTER 1

PREFACE: Is There an Environmental Crisis?

The oil tanker *Exxon Valdez* runs aground and spills millions of gallons of oil into the ocean. A U.S. government agency estimates that there are between 130,000 and 425,000 hazardous waste sites in the United States. The heat waves and droughts of 1988 raise fears that the earth's temperatures are warming because of air pollution. Tropical rain forests are being destroyed, and thousands of species of plants and animals are endangered. Many people believe these different phenomena all prove that there is an environmental crisis.

While almost everyone agrees that pollution exists and that humans have changed the environment, there is controversy over whether there is an environmental crisis. Some people argue that pollution is under control. The environment will improve, they believe, as scientists develop new ways to prevent oil spills, clean up toxic wastes, and reduce the amount of pollution produced by cars and factories. They argue that stories in the media about environmental crises are attempts to scare people.

The next two viewpoints debate whether an environmental crisis exists. As you read them, look for the facts and opinions each presents. Which case is more strongly based on fact, or are they equally factual?

Editor's Note: This viewpoint argues that there is an environmental crisis. It states that pollution is a serious problem that threatens the world. As you read, pay close attention to the facts and opinions used to support this argument.

Of the first four sentences, three are facts and one is an opinion. Can you tell the difference? Identify each.

Is this a fact or an opinion? Why?

This paragraph begins with a statement, then uses facts to support it. Is the statement a fact or opinion?

The magazine *Time* picks a "Person of the Year" at the end of every year. In 1988 the magazine editors instead chose "The Endangered Earth" as "Planet of the Year." On the magazine cover was a globe wrapped in plastic. The picture illustrates the troubles the world faces. These troubles have inspired William D. Ruckelshaus, former head of the Environmental Protection Agency, to call today's situation a "global ecological crisis."

This ecological crisis is caused by pollution. Pollution is the waste humans create and dump into the environment. Some pollution is easy to see. You can see litter in parks and on roadsides, and smog and dirty air in many American cities. You can see garbage that washes up on the shores of many beaches. These are just some of the many kinds of pollution that exist today.

Pollution causes many problems for the world. Sometimes the problems are obvious. Newspapers and television often feature stories on environmental disasters. In Valdez, Alaska, an oil tanker ran into a rock and spilled eleven million gallons of black oil into the ocean. This oil killed fish, seals, and birds and left beaches so dirty it will be years before the oil will be completely washed away.

Copyright 1990, Des Moines Register and Tribune Company. Reprinted with permission.

Pollution can also be less obviously harmful. One example is chlorofluorocarbons (CFCs), which are released by aerosol cans, air conditioners, and some industrial machinery. CFCs are invisible, odorless, and nontoxic. They were thought to be perfectly safe. But now scientists know that they are slowly destroying the ozone in the upper layers of earth's atmosphere. This ozone is important because it protects us from the sun's dangerous ultraviolet rays. Scientists believe CFCs are responsible for the "ozone hole" that was discovered over Antarctica in 1985. People worry that this hole might grow or spread to other parts of the earth.

Is the statement about CFCs a fact or an opinion? Why?

Another form of invisible pollution is the "greenhouse effect." This is caused by gases such as carbon dioxide that let sunlight hit the earth but prevent heat from escaping. The result is that the atmosphere becomes warmer and warmer, just like the inside of a greenhouse.

Air pollution, especially that which results from the burning of oil and coal, has released tons of these gases into the atmosphere. James Hansen of the National Aeronautics and Space Administration argues that carbon dioxide in the earth's atmosphere has risen 30 percent in the past 100 years. He argues that the greenhouse effect caused by carbon dioxide and other air pollution could increase temperatures on the planet by as much as four degrees by the year 2050. Hansen cites as evidence the fact that five of the hottest years in the twentieth century occurred in the 1980s.

What evidence is used to support the existence of the greenhouse effect? Is the evidence based on fact or opinion?

If we do not stop the greenhouse effect, temperatures around the world could get hotter and hotter. The polar ice caps could melt, causing flooding in cities next to oceans. Much of the farmland in countries like the United States could be turned into desert by the rising temperatures.

The earth is the only home we humans have. If we ruin it, there is no other place to go. It is time to recognize that an environmental crisis exists and that something must be done about it.

Is this conclusion a fact or opinion? Why?

How serious is pollution?

Name three types of pollution the author describes. Why does the author believe these types of pollution constitute a crisis?

Editor's Note: This viewpoint argues that pollution is not serious enough to constitute an environmental crisis. As you read, make note of the facts presented in this viewpoint.

Is the author's conclusion in this paragraph a fact or an opinion?

What facts are used to argue that there is no environmental crisis?

Which statements in this paragraph are based on fact? How can you tell?

Many people are worried about the environment. They believe that our land, air and water are becoming so polluted that the U.S. is facing an environmental crisis. They should not be too alarmed. Pollution exists, to be sure, and it would be foolish to ignore it. But to call the present situation an environmental *crisis* is simply wrong.

People who say we have a crisis believe the world is getting more polluted every day. But the amount of pollutants in many American cities has decreased. For example, there are fewer smog alerts in Los Angeles than there used to be. In 1980 Los Angeles had twenty-one serious smog alerts, but in 1987 only one. This improvement in air quality is due in part to the many laws passed in the past two decades to prevent pollution and protect the environment.

There are other reasons to believe that our environment is in good shape. If the environment has worsened, then more people should be ill from the effects. Economist Julian Simon, for example, argues that more people should be dying at a younger age. But statistics show that the average life expectancy of humans is rising in the U.S. and in many other countries. It is at an all-time high of seventy-four years in the U.S. The fact that people are living longer than ever before proves that there is no environmental crisis.

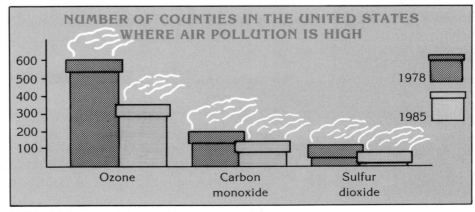

NUMBER OF COUNTIES IN THE UNITED STATES WHERE AIR POLLUTION IS HIGH

600
500
400
300
200
100

Ozone   Carbon   Sulfur
             monoxide   dioxide

1978
1985

SOURCE: U.S. Environmental Protection Agency

Why do some people continue to believe in a crisis? Ben J. Wattenberg, a columnist, has a theory. He writes that humans have a need to worry about something. But the American economy is strong, and the threat of nuclear war seems to be getting smaller, so people worry about the environment instead.

Scientist Hugh W. Ellaesser argues that other scientists exaggerate environmental problems. "There are scientists and environmentalists among us who are less concerned with truth and knowledge than with using scare tactics to secure government research funds," he says. Even scientists exaggerate stories of environmental pollution in order to scare the public into supporting their ideas.

For instance, there has been much talk in the press about the "ozone hole" over Antarctica. It has been blamed on gases called chlorofluorocarbons (CFCs). People argue that these gases destroy the ozone layer in the atmosphere and should be banned. But studies show that the amount of ozone in the atmosphere in the 1960s and 1970s actually grew despite the widespread use of CFCs. So whether banning CFCs would help the ozone layer is still unclear. As for the ozone hole, for all we know it could have existed for years prior to its 1985 discovery. This hole could very well be a natural phenomenon.

Another so-called "crisis" is the greenhouse effect. Scientists such as James Hansen have argued that the droughts and heat waves of recent years are caused by the greenhouse effect. But most of the global warming of this century occurred before 1938, before most of this century's air pollution was produced. So again pollution does not seem to be responsible for the changes in our environment. In fact, no one really knows whether global temperatures will rise or fall in the future. Scientist Richard Lindzen predicts that temperatures over the next century will rise less than one degree, and therefore no global warming crisis exists.

Pollution does exist in the U.S. But the harmful effects of most pollution can be solved with technology and common sense. We are not facing an impending, unsolvable crisis.

SCIENTISTS DISCOVER THE OZONE HOLE

Reprinted with permission of *21st Century Science & Technology*, PO Box 17285, Washington, D.C. 20041.

Is Wattenberg's theory based on fact or opinion? How can you tell?

Of these two statements about the ozone hole, which is a fact? Which is an opinion?

What facts are used to argue against the seriousness of the greenhouse effect?

Is this statement about the ability to cope with pollution a fact or an opinion?

Is there an environmental crisis?

What arguments are given in this viewpoint to prove that pollution does not constitute an environmental crisis? Are these arguments based on fact or opinion?

Tallying the Facts and Opinions

After reading the two viewpoints on the environmental crisis, make a chart similar to the one made for Jim and Laura on page 8. List the facts and opinions each viewpoint gives to support its argument. A chart is started for you below:

Viewpoint 1:

FACTS	OPINIONS
Time magazine picked the earth as "Planet of the Year" in 1988.	The greenhouse effect will cause much of America to become a desert.

Viewpoint 2:

FACTS	OPINIONS
Average life expectancy for Americans is at an all-time high.	Human life expectancy is a good indicator of the health of the environment.

Which article used more factual statements? Which, did you think, was the most convincing? Which one did you personally agree with? Why? List some facts and opinions besides those in the articles that have influenced your opinion.

CHAPTER

PREFACE: Does the U.S. Have a Garbage Crisis?

In 1987 the sea vessel *Mobro* left New York Harbor with 3,168 tons of garbage. It went on a voyage that lasted 6,000 miles and 162 days as six states and three foreign countries refused to let it unload its cargo on their shores. Before the "gar-barge" was finally allowed to land—back in New York—it had become a symbol of what many people called America's garbage crisis.

What can be done with the millions of tons of garbage the U.S. produces every year? William L. Rathje, an archaeologist who studies garbage, states that there are essentially four ways to deal with garbage: dump it, burn it, convert it into something that can be used again (recycling), and minimize the amount of garbage created. The U.S. mostly uses the first two methods. Arguments arise over whether these methods create more problems than they solve and whether more emphasis should be placed on alternatives such as recycling.

The following pair of viewpoints debate the garbage issue. The questions in the margins will help you decide if the statements in these viewpoints are fact or opinion.

Editor's Note: This viewpoint argues that the U.S. is running out of space and methods for disposing of its garbage. It argues that people should reduce the amount of garbage by recycling paper, glass, and other refuse.

Is this a fact or an opinion?

America is a "throwaway" society. Each year Americans throw away 16 billion disposable diapers, 1.6 billion pens, and 220 million tires. For the sake of convenience, we tend to throw these and other used goods away rather than repair or recycle them. The average American household generates 350 bags, or 4,550 gallons, of garbage per year. This comes to a total of 160 million tons of garbage a year. We have to change our throwaway lifestyle before we are buried in it.

We are running out of places to put all the garbage we produce. About 80 percent of it is now buried in landfills. There are 6,000 landfills currently operating, but many of them are becoming full. The Environmental Protection Agency estimates that one-half of the remaining landfills will run out of space and close within the next five-to-ten years.

What facts are used in this paragraph? How might you verify these facts?

Is the answer to this question a fact or an opinion?

Can we simply build new landfills to replace the old ones? The answer is no. For one thing, we are running out of space. We cannot afford to use up land that is needed for farms, parks, and homes.

In addition, many landfills contain toxic chemicals that can leak into and pollute underground water supplies. In New York City, over seventy-five wells had to be closed because of such toxic waste poisoning.

WHAT HAPPENS TO OUR GARBAGE?

83% — Landfills

11% — Recycling

6% — Incineration

SOURCE: National Solid Wastes Management Association, 1986.

One suggested alternative to landfills is to burn the trash. In some states, large incinerators are used to burn garbage, and the heat that is generated is used to produce electricity. But this solution has drawbacks. Burning trash pollutes the air with dioxin and mercury, which are highly poisonous. Furthermore, burning does not completely solve the landfill problem. Leftover ash produced by burning is often highly toxic, and it still has to be buried somewhere.

Are the arguments against burning garbage based on fact or opinion?

The only real solution to the garbage crisis is for Americans to reduce the amount of trash they throw away. There are two methods of doing this. One is recycling—reusing garbage. Bottles can be washed and reused. Aluminum cans can be melted down and remade. Currently in the U.S., only 11 percent of solid waste is used again as something else. Japan, on the other hand, recycles about half of its trash. Environmentalist Barry Commoner estimates that we can reduce 70 percent of our garbage by recyling. In Rhode Island, two automated plants sort out and recycle over 1,000 tons of garbage a day.

Is this a fact or an opinion? Why?

We must also reduce the amount of garbage we produce in the first place. We should use less plastic, which is hard to recycle and does not decompose in landfills. Much garbage is useless packaging. Consumers should buy foods and goods that use less packaging. We also should buy reusable products rather than things that are used once and thrown away. Instead of using and throwing away disposable diapers, for instance, parents should use cloth diapers that can be washed and reused.

Are there any facts in this paragraph? Do you agree with them?

A woman in California was asked about garbage. She replied, "Why do we need to change anything? I put my garbage out on the sidewalk and they take it away." Attitudes like hers must be changed. We have to face the inevitable question posed by Ed Repa, manager of the solid waste disposal program at the National Solid Waste Management Association: "How do you throw something away when there is no 'away'?"

Are these conclusions based on fact or opinion?

Garbage should be recycled

The viewpoint argues that recycling is a better way to reduce garbage than using landfills and incinerators. List three facts and three opinions in this viewpoint that support this argument.

Editor's Note: This viewpoint argues that the U.S. has the capability to safely bury or burn its garbage. It argues that large recycling programs are unnecessary.

Is this a fact or an opinion? Why?

Are Rathje's arguments based on fact or on opinion?

WHAT IS IN OUR GARBAGE?

Glass 9.4%
Metals 9.2%
Other 9.4%
Plastics 6.5%
Paper and Paperboard 42.1%
Food and Yard Waste 23.4%

SOURCE: Franklin Associates

Is America about to be buried in its own garbage? Many people seem to think so and call for Americans to drastically change their lifestyles. But the truth is a bit more complex. The scope of the garbage problem has been exaggerated and distorted.

For one thing, there is no way of measuring precisely how much garbage we produce. No one really knows how many pounds of garbage a person produces per day. Estimates range from three to eight pounds. William L. Rathje, an archaeologist who studies garbage, believes from his research that three pounds is more accurate, and many Americans produce even less garbage.

Rathje has proven that garbage is not a problem. He has studied landfills where garbage is buried. He argues that many items that people think contribute most to the garbage problem are really not so bad. Disposable diapers take up only 1 percent of a landfill's contents. Fast-food packaging takes up one-tenth of 1 percent. Rathje believes plastics in general are not as bad as many people believe. Plastic does not take much space because it can be compressed a great deal. Furthermore, because it does not decompose, plastic cannot leak pollutants into the water or surrounding environment.

People who say there is a garbage crisis argue that we are running out of places to bury it. They argue that half of all landfills currently operating will close within the next five years. But this has always been true about landfills. Most landfills are designed to be used for about ten years. The real problem is that we are not making more.

Why not build new landfills? Are they dangerous? Many landfills now in use, especially older ones, sometimes leak dangerous pollutants into the water supply. But technology can make new landfills leakproof and safe. Are we out of room? Compared to other countries, the U.S. has plenty of space for landfills. The only place where overcrowding is a real problem is in the northeastern states. But even New York state has identified 200 square miles of environmentally safe places for landfill sites.

The real problem is the NIMBY syndrome—Not in My Backyard. Nobody wants to live or work close to a dump. The obstacle to building new landfills is psychological. People must be persuaded to accept landfills as a necessary part of garbage disposal.

Another possible solution is to burn garbage. Japan burns about half of its solid waste in incinerators. People object that incinerators cause more environmental problems than they solve. But available technology can minimize air pollution. Some people argue that burning garbage results in leftover toxic ash that must be buried. But the ash is as safe to bury as ordinary garbage, and it takes up much less space. Critics of incinerators are just another example of the NIMBY syndrome. The U.S. should also build more incinerators, especially in locations where landfill sites are truly scarce.

Name one fact and one opinion the author uses to support the incineration of garbage.

Many people believe that recycling can solve the garbage problem. But recycling has both economic and practical limits. Paper, for example, can be recycled only twice. The National Solid Waste Management Association has estimated that we can recycle only 25 percent of our garbage. So we will still need landfills and incinerators.

To conclude, America has a garbage management problem that can be solved by the prudent use of available methods and technologies. The U.S. does not have a crisis, and Americans do not have to feel so guilty about the garbage they are producing.

Are the conclusions of this viewpoint facts or opinions? Do you agree with them?

Landfills and incinerators

The viewpoint argues that landfills and incinerators can deal with America's garbage and that it is the public's opinion that must be changed. Do you agree with the author? Why or why not?

Would you like a landfill or incinerator built close to where you live? Why or why not? Provide some facts or opinions to support your answer.

2 Distinguishing Between Fact and Opinion

This activity will allow you to practice distinguishing between fact and opinion. The statements below focus on the subject matter of this chapter, whether America faces a garbage problem. Read each statement and consider it carefully. *Mark O for any statement you believe is an opinion, or what one person believes to be true. Mark F for any statement you believe is a fact, or something that can be proven to be true. Mark U for any statement for which you cannot decide.*

EXAMPLE: Landfills are worse than incinerators.

ANSWER: Opinion: this statement expresses one person's opinion. Others would disagree.

Answer

1. America generates millions of tons of trash every week. _____

2. America produces too much garbage. _____

3. In West Germany the government has declared over 35,000 waste sites as potentially harmful to the environment. _____

4. About 80 percent of trash in the U.S. is buried in landfills. _____

5. Some cities use garbage incinerators to generate electricity. _____

6. Recycling will not work because people are too lazy to sort their trash. _____

7. Landfills built today are totally leakproof and safe. _____

8. Plastic does not decompose in landfills. _____

9. Plastic is good because it does not decompose and release harmful chemicals into landfills. _____

3

PREFACE: Is Acid Rain a Serious Problem?

Acid rain is rain, snow, or other precipitation that contains high levels of sulfuric or nitric acids. It is formed when sulfur dioxide and nitrogen oxide combine with moisture in the air. Acid rain has been blamed for killing fish and other aquatic wildlife, harming trees, and damaging buildings and monuments. Though first described by the British chemist Robert Angus Smith in the 1800s, acid rain has become an internationally recognized problem only in the last two decades. The areas most affected by acid rain include the northeastern United States, Canada, Scandinavia, Germany, and the Soviet Union. Much disagreement exists, however, over the causes of acid rain and over how harmful it is.

These controversies exist because the effects of acid rain develop slowly. Pollution from one location might affect lakes hundreds of miles away over a period of years. Disagreements also arise over acid rain because proposed measures to combat it, such as installing scrubbers in power plants, can cost billions of dollars. Questions remain as to whether such expensive measures would solve the problem.

The following two viewpoints present opposing arguments on acid rain.

VIEWPOINT 5 Acid rain is a serious problem

Editor's Note: The following viewpoint argues that acid rain is a serious problem caused by pollution. Pay attention to the facts and opinions used to describe the causes and effects of acid rain.

Are the opening statements of this viewpoint facts or opinions? How can you tell?

Is this a factual description of acid rain?

One of the most serious environmental problems facing the U.S. today is acid rain. Acid rain harms our lakes, our forests, and our health.

Acid rain is caused by sulfur dioxide and nitrogen oxide. These gases combine with water in the atmosphere to form sulfuric and nitric acids. These acids then return to earth in the form of rain, snow, and fog.

Sulfur dioxide is formed by metal smelters and coal- and oil-fired power plants. Nitrogen oxides are emitted by automobiles and factories. Both sulfur dioxide and nitrogen oxide are also formed by natural means, such as volcanos and forest fires. This has led some people to claim that nature causes acid rain. But this is not the case. In the eastern half of the United States, for

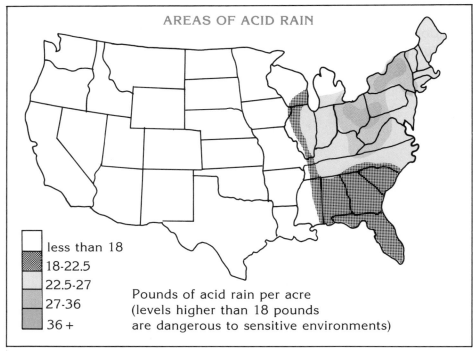

AREAS OF ACID RAIN

less than 18
18-22.5
22.5-27
27-36
36+

Pounds of acid rain per acre
(levels higher than 18 pounds
are dangerous to sensitive environments)

SOURCE: Canadian Government

example, factories, cars, and other pollution sources have dumped about thirty million tons of sulfur dioxide into the atmosphere. Natural sources have added less than one million tons. According to biophysicist Roy Gould, more than 90 percent of the nitrogen oxides in the eastern half of the United States have come from artificial sources. Clearly, pollution causes far more acid rain in the United States than natural sources.

How harmful are these acids? They kill lakes by making them so acidic that fish cannot survive in them. Canada's Department of the Environment has stated that 14,000 of its lakes have no fish in them because of acid rain. They also predict that 150,000 more lakes are dying. In the United States, 212 lakes in the Adirondacks in New York are dead, and 9,000 are endangered, according to the Worldwatch Institute.

Acid rain also weakens and destroys forests. Acid rain causes the leaves and needles of trees to fall off. This makes trees weak and vulnerable to disease. In Germany the famous Black Forest is dying. Trees and forests are also threatened in Central Europe, Scandinavia, Canada, and the United States.

Finally, acid rain poses a direct threat to human health. This is because the air pollutants that cause acid rain also damage the lungs. Philip J. Landrigan, a professor of community medicine and pediatrics, argues that acid rain is the third largest cause of lung disease. Children and the elderly are especially vulnerable to air pollution. In addition, acid rain allows toxic substances like lead, cadmium, and asbestos to seep into the drinking water. One study estimated that acid rain is responsible for 50,000 deaths a year in the U.S.

Acid rain is a silent killer. We must stop the pollution that causes acid rain before it does more damage to our environment.

Is this statement a fact or opinion?

Is the statement about 14,000 lakes a fact or an opinion? Why?

Is this a fact or an opinion?

Is this a fact or an opinion?

The harm done by acid rain

This viewpoint argues that certain kinds of air pollution can lead to dead lakes and forests. How? Name three ways acid rain affects the environment, according to the author.

Editor's Note: The following viewpoint gives several arguments to prove that acid rain is not a problem. Pay attention to the facts and opinions used to support the arguments.

Can you find an opinion in this paragraph?

Is the first statement a fact or an opinion?

Is this conclusion a fact or an opinion?

Is acid rain as bad as many people say? There is plenty of evidence that shows it is not. There is reason to question whether 1) pollution causes acid rain, 2) whether acid rain really harms lakes in the U.S. and Canada, and 3) whether acid rain harms human health.

Acid rain is caused when moisture in the atmosphere combines with certain chemicals to become acidic. Many people say that this acidity is caused by cars and industry. But *all* rain is naturally acidic.

The two chemicals responsible for acid rain, sulfur dioxide and nitrogen oxide, have many natural sources. The decay in swamps, coastlines, and other shallow-water areas produces these chemicals. Lightning adds nitric acid to the air. And volcanos spew out acidic materials into the atmosphere. After the eruption of Mt. St. Helens in Washington in May 1980, measurements of sulfur dioxide in the surrounding atmosphere went from 40 tons per day before the eruption to 500-3,400 tons per day for several months after it. Some geologists have estimated that volcanos emit about 100 million tons of sulfur compounds per year. So even if we stopped using cars and electrical plants, acid rain would still be with us.

ACID RAIN DOES NOT PRODUCE ACID LAKES

	Amount of Acid Rain (Adirondacks = 100)	Percent of Acid Lakes	Percent of Lake Area That Is Acid
Adirondacks	100	10.1	1.7
Michigan Upper Peninsula	50	9.4	2.4
Florida	15	12.4	12.0
Frazer Island, Australia	0	79.0	98.0

SOURCE: U.S. Department of Energy, 1989.

Even when acid rain occurs, there is no clear evidence that it increases the acidity of lakes. Edward Krug, who works for the Illinois Water Survey, concludes that the amount of acid rain has little to do with the acidity of a lake. For example, even though Florida's rain is less acidic than that in the Adirondacks, lakes in Florida have higher acidity. Krug argues that most of their water in lakes is runoff from roads and fields. Water gets its acidity from these sources, Krug argues, and not from pollution in the air.

Is this evidence factual? Why or why not?

Does acid rain harm forests? Scientists are not sure. Dying forests could be a natural phenomenon, or they could have a wide variety of causes, such as drought, pests, or other pollutants. The decline of red spruce in the Appalachian Mountains has been blamed on acid rain. But a similar decline in red spruce occurred between 1871 and 1890, before acid rain was a problem. A 1987 U.S. government report on acid rain argued that sulfur dioxide was not harming crops or forests.

What evidence is presented to prove acid rain may not harm forests? Is it based on fact or opinion?

Does acid rain threaten human health? There is little scientific evidence to support this claim. Several scientific surveys have not found any link between sulfur and nitrogen oxide pollution and unsafe air or drinking water. Some newspaper articles quote the figure of 50,000 annual deaths caused by acid rain, but that is just a guess.

Panic over acid rain is based on biased opinion, not on fact. Only by looking at this issue objectively can we learn the facts about acid rain.

Is acid rain harmful?

This viewpoint presents three main arguments. It argues that air pollution does not cause acid rain, that acid rain does not cause acid lakes, and that acid rain does not harm human health. Do you agree? After reading this viewpoint and the opposing view, which one do you find more convincing? Why?

Understanding Editorial Cartoons

Throughout this book you have seen cartoons that illustrate the ideas in the viewpoints. Editorial cartoons are an effective and usually humorous way of presenting an opinion on an issue. While many cartoons are easy to understand, others, like the one below, may require more thought.

The cartoon below is similar to the cartoons that appear in your daily newspaper. It deals with acid rain. The man with the briefcase labeled EPA represents the Environmental Protection Agency, the U.S. government department responsible for keeping America's water and air clean.

Look at the cartoon. Why is the skeleton in the cartoon? What do you think is the cartoonist's opinion of the EPA? How can you tell? Do you think that the cartoonist believes acid rain is a serious problem? Why? Do you think the cartoon is funny? Why or why not?

© Liederman/Rothco

CHAPTER

PREFACE: Is the Earth Running Out of Resources?

In 1980 a group of scientists and economists commissioned by President Jimmy Carter issued *Global 2000 Report to the President.* The report concluded that "if present trends continue, the world in 2000 will be more crowded, more polluted, less stable ecologically. . .than the world we live in now. Serious stresses involving population, resources, and environment are clearly visible ahead." The report argued that growing overpopulation was consuming the earth's resources and destroying the environment.

In 1984 economist Julian L. Simon and futurist Herman Kahn came out with *The Resourceful Earth,* a response to *Global 2000.* Working with much of the same statistical data, they concluded that the original report was "dead wrong." Simon, Kahn, and others argue that the earth has enough resources to support even more people.

Today the debate continues over whether the earth's resources are running out. The following two viewpoints represent the opposite sides of this debate.

> **Editor's Note:** This viewpoint argues that a future environmental crisis could develop as humans continue to deplete the earth's limited resources. Pay close attention to the facts and opinions presented.

Are the statements describing the earth facts or opinions?

Is this a fact or an opinion? Why?

When Americans first landed on the moon, one of the most famous photographs taken was that of the earth. The planet looked small, beautiful, and vulnerable. Geologist Preston Cloud wrote "Mother Earth will never seem the same again. No more can thinking people take this little planet. . .as an infinite theater of action and provider of resources for man." The resources of our planet are not endless. But people still live as if they were.

We are all consumers and are all dependent on our environment. We depend on our small planet for the air we breathe, the water we drink, the food we eat, the energy to keep us warm, and the materials for all our possessions. The environmental crisis ultimately boils down to the fact that there are too many people in the world consuming too many resources.

One factor facing the world is our exploding population. It took until 1800 to reach a global population of one billion people. It reached two billion in 1930, four billion in 1975, and stands at

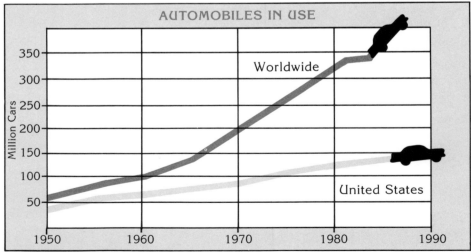

SOURCE: Motor Vehicles Manufacturers Association, 1988.

over five billion today. It is expected to reach over ten billion early in the next century. Population continues to grow rapidly, especially in poor parts of the world such as Africa. Our population has reached a crisis level. Every additional person born puts more strain on the earth's resources.

The problem is not just the number of people but the amount of resources they consume. The United States, with only 5 percent of the world's population, uses 25 percent of the world's resources. This is in part because of our wasteful lifestyle. We love our cars, which are a major cause of air pollution and the greenhouse effect. Americans generate a ton of trash per person each year. Ninety-six percent of the energy used by the U.S. is taken from resources such as oil, wood, and natural gas. These resources cannot be replaced once they are used up. People in America and other wealthy countries are the main culprits in depleting the earth's resources.

Paul Ehrlich, who wrote *The Population Bomb,* compares humanity's situation with that of a family who spends more money than it makes. After a while, the family's savings are gone, and a crisis develops. The "savings" we are consuming now are the earth's resources. The soil we depend on for farming, the underground fresh water, and the fossil fuels of coal and oil—all took thousands or millions of years to form. When they are gone, they cannot be instantly replaced, and we will really be in trouble.

We have to change the way we live. This means paying attention to little things, such as turning off the lights when we leave a room and recycling bottles and newspapers. It means walking or finding other alternatives to transportation by automobile. It means learning to live with fewer possessions. Countries will have to change as well and learn to cooperate more, because the resource crisis is a global problem. We must protect our earth for the generations to come.

Is this a fact or an opinion? Why?

What point is being made about the American lifestyle? Is this a fact or an opinion?

Scott Long. Reprint by permission of the *Star Tribune.*

Is this statement a fact or an opinion?

Is this conclusion a fact or an opinion? Why?

Running out?

The viewpoint argues that the human population is consuming too many of earth's resources and that these resources are in danger of running out.

Do you believe the earth is running out of resources? What reasons would you give for your opinion?

Editor's Note: This viewpoint argues that the earth has plenty of resources to support the growing human population. It argues that humans are capable of discovering and developing new resources as they become needed. Consider the evidence the author supplies to support this view. Is it based on fact or opinion?

Warnings about overpopulation and using up natural resources are nothing new. In the days of the Roman empire, people claimed that population growth was too great and that the earth was worn out. More recently, in the 1930s, some educators were telling students that the world's fuel supplies would soon be exhausted and they would be living in the dark. Of course they were wrong. Today the world's proven oil reserves are bigger than ever before. We have barely touched the earth's resources.

Is this a fact or an opinion?

When people say we are running out of resources, they are forgetting something. They are forgetting that humans are clever. Humans will find new resources and substitutes, especially in societies like the United States. For instance, in the seventeenth century the English worried about an impending shortage of wood.

Are these historical examples facts or opinions? How can you tell?

Reprinted by permission of UFS, Inc.

This led to the development of coal as a substitute. Then in the 1800s they worried about running out of coal. This led to the discovery and development of oil. In the future, solar and nuclear energy will be developed and used. History shows that resources do not really run out because we can come up with new ones.

Jacqueline Kasun, a professor of economics, states that resources are virtually limitless. No more than 1 to 3 percent of the land is occupied by humans, and humans use only one-ninth of the earth's ice-free land for farming. The earth could support over twenty times the people it does now. This would still leave half the world's land surface to nature, according to Kasun. Economist Max Singer has stated that the earth could support twenty billion people and still avoid an environmental crisis.

People who worry about overpopulation view every person as a consumer. But as economist Julian Simon argues, people are not just consumers. They are also producers and contributors to society. A large population leads to more solutions, not problems. Simon argues that the most important resource is the human mind. And "when there are more people, there are more productive minds."

Environmentalists are trying to make us feel guilty. They are saying the rich, wastefully consuming Americans are the problem, and they want to force us to lead simpler, poorer lives. But we can learn to manage our environment and enrich our lives without having to become organic farmers.

What reasons does Kasun give to support her belief that the earth has enough resources? Are her views based on fact or opinion?

Is this quotation a fact or an opinion?

Is this a fact or an opinion?

Are humans the problem or the solution?

This viewpoint argues the earth is not running out of resources. Why?

After reading both viewpoints, do you believe we need to change the way we live in order to preserve the environment? Why or why not?

4

Using Facts to Support Opinions

The viewpoints in this book all attempt to persuade the reader. To do this, the author may point out facts to support his or her opinion. A well-constructed essay will always supply the reader with enough evidence to evaluate the argument. This is why it is very important to learn to construct paragraphs that include factual information to support the topic sentence.

In this exercise, you will be asked to write a paragraph that uses facts to support an opinion. Below are listed some statements along with some supporting evidence. You will be asked to write a paragraph using the information provided.

EXAMPLE: Opinion: The use of cars should be restricted.

Facts: Cars consume petroleum.
Petroleum is a nonrenewable resource.
Petroleum sometimes is spilled in the ocean.
Cars release carbon dioxide to the atmosphere.
Carbon dioxide contributes to global warming.
There are 400 million cars in operation worldwide.

Now, these facts are used in a paragraph to support the main idea.

We should restrict our use of cars. The 400 million automobiles used in the world today both consume natural resources and pollute the environment. Automobiles release large amounts of carbon dioxide into the air, which is a main cause of global warming. By promoting bicycles and mass transit instead of automobiles, we can conserve our oil resources and make the world a better place to live.

Now write your own paragraph similar to the above example. Pick one of the two opinions listed below as your topic sentence, then use the facts to support it. You may also select facts from the viewpoints. Make sure to select facts that support your opinion.

Opinions (topic sentence): Population growth is a major problem.
Population growth is not a major problem.

Facts: The 1990 world population is 5.3 billion people.
The world added around 90 million people in 1989.
Around 800 million people are starving.
Japan is a wealthy and densely populated country.
Bangladesh is a poor and densely populated country.
Each year over a million acres of swamps and deserts are converted into cropland.
A United Nations study concluded that Africa could grow food for ten billion people.
Africa, which has most of the world's starving people, has the highest population growth rate in the world.